Brilliant Activities for

Creative Writing, Year 3

Activities for Developing Writing Composition Skills

Irene Yates

Brilliant
PUBLICATIONS

We hope you and your pupils enjoy using the ideas in this book. Brilliant Publications publishes many other books to help primary school teachers. To find out more details on all of our titles, including those listed below, please log onto our website: www.brilliantpublications.co.uk.

Other books in the Brilliant Activities for Creative Writing Series

Year 1	978-0-85747-463-6
Year 2	978-0-85747-464-3
Year 4	978-0-85747-466-7
Year 5	978-0-85747-467-4
Year 6	978-0-85747-468-1

Boost Creative Writing Series – Planning Sheets to Support Writers (Especially SEN Pupils)

Years 1–2	978-1-78317-058-6
Years 3–4	978-1-78317-059-3
Years 5–6	978-1-78317-060-9

Brilliant Activities for Reading Comprehension Series

Year 1	978-1-78317-070-8
Year 2	978-1-78317-071-5
Year 3	978-1-78317-072-2
Year 4	978-1-78317-073-9
Year 5	978-1-78317-074-6
Year 6	978-1-78317-075-3

Published by Brilliant Publications
Unit 10
Sparrow Hall Farm
Edlesborough
Dunstable
Bedfordshire
LU6 2ES, UK

Email: info@brilliantpublications.co.uk
Website: www.brilliantpublications.co.uk
Tel: 01525 222292

The name Brilliant Publications and the logo are registered trademarks.

Written by Irene Yates
Illustrated by Carol Jonas
Front cover illustration by Carol Jonas

Printed ISBN 978-0-85747-465-0
e-book ISBN 978-0-85747-472-8

First printed and published in the UK in 2014

The right of Irene Yates to be identified as the author of this work has been asserted by herself in accordance with the Copyright, Designs and Patents Act 1988.

Contents

Introduction

The Brilliant Activities for Creative Writing series is designed to stimulate developing writers to access the National Curriculum Programmes of Study for writing composition.

Each book contains practice activities to assist pupils in understanding, revising and consolidating their skills in writing. The activities are structured to help each pupil to understand how to:

- write for a widening range of purposes and audiences
- organize ideas into coherent and grammatically correct sentences
- improve, and make progress in, their own writing
- increase their accuracy in the use of punctuation
- develop their knowledge and confidence in spelling
- use and enlarge their writing vocabulary
- write in different ways for different genres and types of text
- develop their own way with words

The sheets are structured but flexible so that they can be used alone or as follow-ons. The ideas on the sheets can all be used as a basis for more lessons for reinforcement purposes. Each book aims to offer:

- a range of familiar text forms
- a range of appropriate contexts
- opportunities to experiment with words drawn from language experience, literature and media
- opportunities to select vocabulary according to demands of activity
- use of proof-reading, checking and editing, sharing with peers
- encouragement to pupils to reflect upon their understanding of the writing process

Each activity is fully explained and the teacher tip boxes give hints and suggestions for making the most of them or for follow-up activities. No additional resources are necessary, other than writing implements and extra paper for more extended writing where it is appropriate. Children should be encouraged to talk about what they are going to write, prior to writing, with a partner, in groups or as a class. Discussing what they want to write, prior to doing so, will help them to structure their thoughts and ideas. Through careful questioning, adults can help children to develop their vocabulary and understanding of how language works.

Obviously, all of the activities would work well if the children are able to word process on a computer at some times – this would be an added bonus.

It is hoped that this series of books will encourage pupils to use their writing to reflect upon and monitor their own learning, to encourage them to read as writers and to write as readers and, more than anything else, to learn to write with joy.

Brilliant Activities for Creative Writing, Year 3
© Irene Yates and Brilliant Publications

Links to the curriculum

The sheets in **Brilliant Activities for Creative Writing** will help Year 3 pupils to develop their composition skills, as set out in the National Curriculum for England (2014).

Composition

The sheets in **Brilliant Activities for Creative Writing** help pupils to plan their writing, by providing a structured format for discussing and recording their ideas. Pupils should also be given the opportunity to read and discuss other pieces of writing, so that they learn from the structure, vocabulary and grammar.

Composing and rehearsing sentences orally, prior to writing, helps pupils to build a varied and rich vocabulary and encourages an increased range of sentence structures. Talking through what they want to say will also help pupils to become aware of when they should start a new paragraph. The Tip boxes at the bottom of each sheet provide starting points for discussions.

The activities support pupils in developing settings, characters and plot in their narrative writing. Those sheets focusing on non-narrative writing introduce the use of simple organizational devises such as headings and bullet points. The Plan sheets (pages 43–46) will help them to focus on the features particular to each type of writing.

When pupils have finished their writing, they should be encouraged to re-read their work and to think about how it can be improved. Discussing their work with you and with other pupils will help them to assess the effectiveness of their own writing.

Reading their writing aloud helps children to see that their writing is valued. Encourage pupils to use appropriate intonation and to control the tone and volume so that the meaning clear.

Vocabulary, grammar and punctuation

Many of the sheets can be used to reinforce children's understanding of grammar and punctuation, but this is not the primary purpose of the sheets. Many sheets contain Word boxes to encourage children to extend their range of vocabulary and prompt them to use new words in their writing.

The following sheets deal with particular grammar and punctuation points:

- The real 'You' and What's fun (pages 7–8) – using first and third person voice
- Whose dream? (page 11) – adverbs
- Best place ever, What makes you angry?, Build your confidence and In the rainforest (pages 12, 18, 21 and 39) – adjectives
- Can you … ? (page 15) – use of the indefinite articles 'a' and 'an'
- What makes you smile? (page 16) – parts of speech
- What makes you laugh? (page 17) – conjunctions
- Magic powers (page 22) – prepositions
- Picture this (page 25) – speech marks
- Three-legged race (page 28) – using second person voice
- Dead Man's Island (page 29) – verbs

Your story

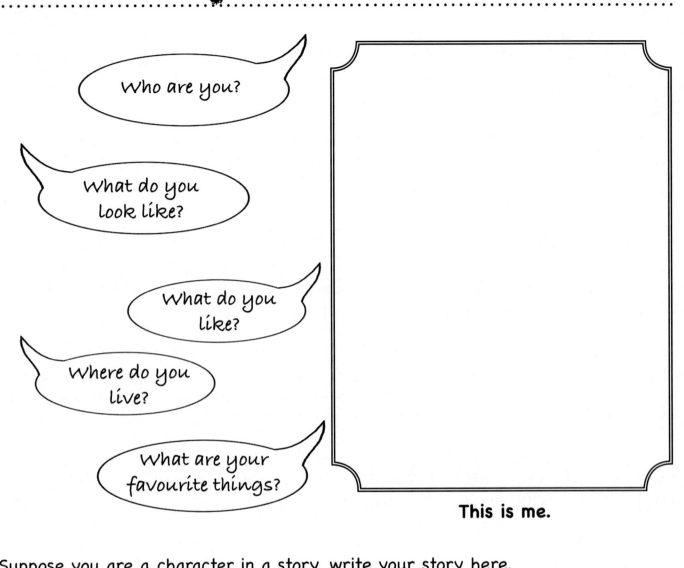

This is me.

Suppose you are a character in a story, write your story here.

Remind the children that the story needs a beginning, a middle and an end. Can they turn their character into a hero or heroine?

Brilliant Activities for Creative Writing, Year 3
© Irene Yates and Brilliant Publications

The real 'You'

Is that really me?

Pretend you are somebody else writing a biography about you. What do you think they would say?

Think up a list of questions for an interview and the answers that you would give.

Write your biography here.

Remember:

This is a biography, not an autobiography. Don't use 'I', 'me' or 'my' words.

Lots of discussion to help writers step out of the 'self' box and be objective. Focus on pronouns being consistent with the verbs.

What's fun?

Write a personal journal, telling us about all the things you love and why.

Personal journal

Remember:
Write your journal in the first person; 'I', and the present tense.

Assist with discussion. Focus on personal pronoun and tense of verbs. Writer to check when piece is finished.

Brilliant Activities for Creative Writing, Year 3
© Irene Yates and Brilliant Publications

Who cares?

Have a discussion with your friends to find out about all the different things that people care about. Now decide what's important to you. Show **what** you care about and **why** you care about it.

_____

_____

_____

_____

_____

_____

_____

Lots of talk please! Explore ideas, encourage the children to make notes and draft out. Read and check.

How to be perfect

Have a discussion with your friends. What makes the perfect friend/person/pet/teacher/game? What qualities would make somebody perfect? Talk about it first and then write a set of rules for 'How to be Perfect'.

Remember:
Use bullet points. Look back at the ideas/notes you have talked about.

Focus on talk. Encourage making notes of the key points/words and ideas. Re-cap the use of bullet points for making a list. Encourage humorous writing.

Brilliant Activities for Creative Writing, Year 3
© Irene Yates and Brilliant Publications

Whose dream?

Suppose you have a dream come true.
Talk about it with your group/friends.
What would your dream be?
Discuss what might happen.
Plan and write the story.

A dream come true.

If only I ...

Old Trafford

Try:
Use some of these adverbs in your story:

| then | next | soon | happily | somewhere | usually |

Lots of talk. Encourage note-taking and writing down key words and ideas. Re-cap the given adverbs and award extra kudos for using them correctly.

Best place ever

Sit down in a group and take it in turns to say, as many places as you can that you think are great. Take notes of your friends' answers. Choose your favourite answer; this could be a setting for a story. Think it through and work out what might happen, write a description of this place.

My chosen place

Try:
Make a list of some really good adjectives that might be useful for your description.

Give lots of time for exploring verbally. Encourage lots of spoken description. Re-cap adjectives. Write down key words and ideas.

Brilliant Activities for Creative Writing, Year 3
© Irene Yates and Brilliant Publications

What if ... ?

Talk in your group about 'not fitting in', or 'being the odd one out'. Discuss ideas about how to make sure everyone is included.

What if I don't fit in?

Write the story of the child in the picture, using some of the ideas you have talked about today.

_ _

_ _

_ _

_ _

_ _

_ _

_ _

_ _

_ _

_ _

_ _

Focus on talking and swapping ideas, exploring problems and solutions and personal feelings.

Loneliness

Work in pairs to write a play script.

Who?

Where?

What?

Why?

When?

How?

Think:
Make sure you know what a play script looks like.

Plan by reading through a play script. Divide children into pairs. Create characters, settings, problems and solutions. Practise dialogue before they begin to write. Read/act out aloud.

Brilliant Activities for Creative Writing, Year 3
© Irene Yates and Brilliant Publications

Can you ... ?

Write a poem without using the word 'a'?

Here's an example:

An elephant
Had an interesting
Dream about
An expedition to
Another land but
Found his trunk was
Just too heavy
To carry.

- -

- -

- -

- -

- -

- -

- -

- -

Try:
Turn the example poem into one that can only use 'a' and not 'an'.
How can you do that?

Discuss the 'a' and 'an' rule with words beginning with a vowel or a consonant. Lots of talking and exploring ideas before writing.

What makes you smile?

This is what makes me smile.

Nouns	Verbs	Proper nouns
friends	to play with ...	James, from next door
- - - - - - -	- - - - - - -	- - - - - - -
- - - - - - -	- - - - - - -	- - - - - - -
- - - - - - -	- - - - - - -	- - - - - - -

These things make me laugh:

Nouns	Verbs	Proper nouns
- - - - - - -	- - - - - - -	- - - - - - -
- - - - - - -	- - - - - - -	- - - - - - -
- - - - - - -	- - - - - - -	- - - - - - -
- - - - - - -	- - - - - - -	- - - - - - -

Recap on nouns, verbs and proper nouns. Lots of examples through discussion.

Brilliant Activities for Creative Writing, Year 3
© Irene Yates and Brilliant Publications

What makes you laugh?

Think of six things that have made you laugh recently. Write them in the boxes below.

Share them with your friends. Have a competition – who used the most conjunctions? Which was the funniest?

Try:
Use these conjunctions if you can: when, so, after, while, because, but

Work on practising brevity and using conjunctions. Lots of discussion before and after writing.

What makes you angry?

Write about three things that have made you really cross.

-------------------------------------   -------------------------------------

-------------------------------------   -------------------------------------

-------------------------------------   -------------------------------------

-------------------------------------   -------------------------------------

-------------------------------------   -------------------------------------

-------------------------------------   -------------------------------------

Try:
Use these adjectives if you can: early, difficult, regular, popular, busy, fine.

General discussion about how it feels when you are angry. Explore ideas for stimulus. Re-cap adjectives.

Brilliant Activities for Creative Writing, Year 3
© Irene Yates and Brilliant Publications

My specialist subject

Write a two minute talk on your special interest.
This is the ultimate show and tell. Write your talk
so that you can read it to 'impress' your friends and
classmates.

I love dancing

I collect fossils

I'm great on a trampoline

Remember:
You will need to write for more than two minutes to have two minutes of speech.

Make sure everyone has something to write about. Plug self-esteem and pride. Organize a reading of the talks and then a feedback session for discussion of interests.

Who do you admire?

Have a discussion with your friends about the different people you admire. Why are these people admired?

- -

- -

Choose a person that you admire, write a description of them and give reasons why you admire this person. Share with the group and give comments and ideas for the writing.

- -

- -

- -

- -

- -

- -

- -

Try:
Write in paragraphs. Aim for three; one to introduce your subject, one to discuss and one to sum up.

Lots of discussion to get ideas flowing. Focus on the reading out and group feedback.

Brilliant Activities for Creative Writing, Year 3
© Irene Yates and Brilliant Publications

Build your confidence

Create a confidence chart. Use an adjective for each letter of the alphabet.

a. _____   b. _____

c. _____   d. _____

e. _____   f. _____

g. _____   h. _____

i. _____   j. _____

k. _____   l. _____

m. _____   n. _____

o. _____   p. _____

q. _____   r. _____

s. _____   t. _____

u. _____   v. _____

w. _____   x. _____

y. _____

z. _____

If you can't find a word for any letters, use a word that contains that letters eg for x =ex<u>x</u>citable

Remember:
Only use positive words – you can be as funny as you like.

Re-cap 'adjective'. Talk after the writing is done. Enjoy!

Magic powers

What magic power would you like?

Use as many of these prepositions as you can to write a story:
on; by; to; of; as; at; after; but; by; down; through; with.

Have a mind-mapping session. Encourage noting down of key words and phrases. Lots of talk before writing about their chosen magic power.

Brilliant Activities for Creative Writing, Year 3
© Irene Yates and Brilliant Publications

Put yourself in their shoes

Pretend you are someone else that you have read about or seen in a movie or on TV;

Okay. I choose ...

Now tell your story as him/her.

Remember:
Where you can, organize your writing into paragraphs.

Discussion of pronouns and how verbs change when the pronoun is different. Talk about proof-reading to make sure the pronoun hasn't changed halfway through the story.

Write to read

Which story do you know well?

Re-tell the story here – you are going to read this out to your group, so make it the very best you can do.

Give plenty of examples, so that every child has a choice. Focus on exploring ideas and getting them down in a form to be read aloud. Organize readings and constructive and positive feedback.

Brilliant Activities for Creative Writing, Year 3
© Irene Yates and Brilliant Publications

Picture this

"This is my family on holiday. What happens next?"

Remember:
Use inverted commas (speech marks) for when they are talking to each other.
Give them all names.

Lots of talk to explore and develop ideas. Develop concept of direct speech using speech marks.

Be a hero

Write what happens from all three points-of-view: the child – the hero; the old man – saved in time; and the car driver who almost caused an accident.

Think:
How would each person feel?

Talk through what did/could have happened. Explain how different characters will have different perceptions. Discuss and then write descriptions of different emotions.

Brilliant Activities for Creative Writing, Year 3
© Irene Yates and Brilliant Publications

Three's a crowd

Write the story. Start with the third monster butting in and causing a difficult situation.

Remember:
Plan your story. Write in the past tense. Introduce characters, time and place.
Build a problem. Give a resolution. Check and edit.

Lots of talk to explore ideas. Go through the process of writing the narrative.

Three-legged race

Write your instructions for winning the race. Think about what is needed and the rules for the race. Use plenty of action verbs like tie, walk, run. Check your usage of adjectives, pronouns and verb tenses.

Design a poster titled 'How to run with three legs'.

Think:
Can you use second person voice 'YOU'?

Show some written instructions as a model for the poster. Practise as a whole group with an easy situation like 'How to make a sandwich.'

Brilliant Activities for Creative Writing, Year 3
© Irene Yates and Brilliant Publications

Dead Man's Island

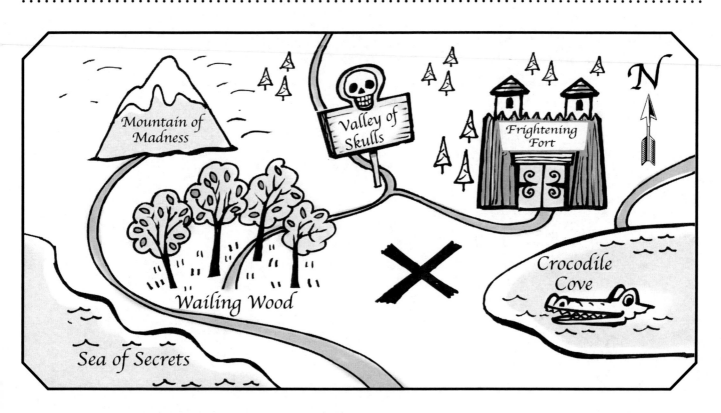

Write instructions for finding the treasure.

Think about:
What equipment the treasure seekers need. How they can get across the island. Directions they must go in. The forms of transport they might need.

Words to help
sail, trek climb, row, fly, swim, avoid, fight, watch out, dig, spade, boat, ship, treasure

Use scrap paper for planning. Focus on interesting action verbs and clear sequencing. Explain compass points.

What a day!

That day in the playground, we were all racing about when, suddenly ...

Write notes:

Try:
Jot down all the key words that will prompt your flow of ideas, then form them into a story.

Lots of talk. Take all ideas into the melting pot and explore and develop.

Brilliant Activities for Creative Writing, Year 3
© Irene Yates and Brilliant Publications

How to do almost anything

How do I learn to ride a bike?

By practising!

How do I learn to kick a football?

By practising!

How do I learn to play the guitar?

By practising!

How do I learn to write?

By practising!

By practising!

Write for five minutes without stopping your hand from moving. You can write about anything. Don't stop to think, just write! Use the back of this sheet if necessary.

Discuss how skills are learned and practised until they are effective. Have daily five minute sessions of 'without thinking' writing.

Let me persuade you!

All children should
learn to play a musical
instrument.

Yes, I think we
should because ...

No, I don't think
so, because ...

What do you think? Do you agree or disagree?
What arguments can you put forward to support
your point-of-view (for or against)? Find at least
three.

----

*Persuasive text needs to be written in the present tense and in the first person. Each point should start with a new paragraph.
Stress logical sequence.*

Brilliant Activities for Creative Writing, Year 3
© Irene Yates and Brilliant Publications

My favourite trip

Write a recount of your best trip ever. Think about the order of things before you write:

- who was there
- where you were
- what you did
- why you went
- what happened.

Finish with a comment about your trip.

Try:
Use these conjunctives if you can:
first
next
the
lastly
finally

Focus on thinking and making notes, sequencing events and using paragraphs. Remind them to write in the first person and in the past tense.

Sandwiches, glorious sandwiches!

How do I make a sandwich?

First choose your sandwich filling: chicken, ham, beef, egg, cheese, lettuce, tomato, cucumber, your choice?

Equipment needed:

- -

- -

Ingredients required:

- -

- -

Method:

- -

- -

- -

- -

- -

- -

- -

Now eat and enjoy!

Lots of talk about sandwich making: varying ingredients and utensils required. Focus on the sequencing of instructions.

Brilliant Activities for Creative Writing, Year 3
© Irene Yates and Brilliant Publications

What can you write?

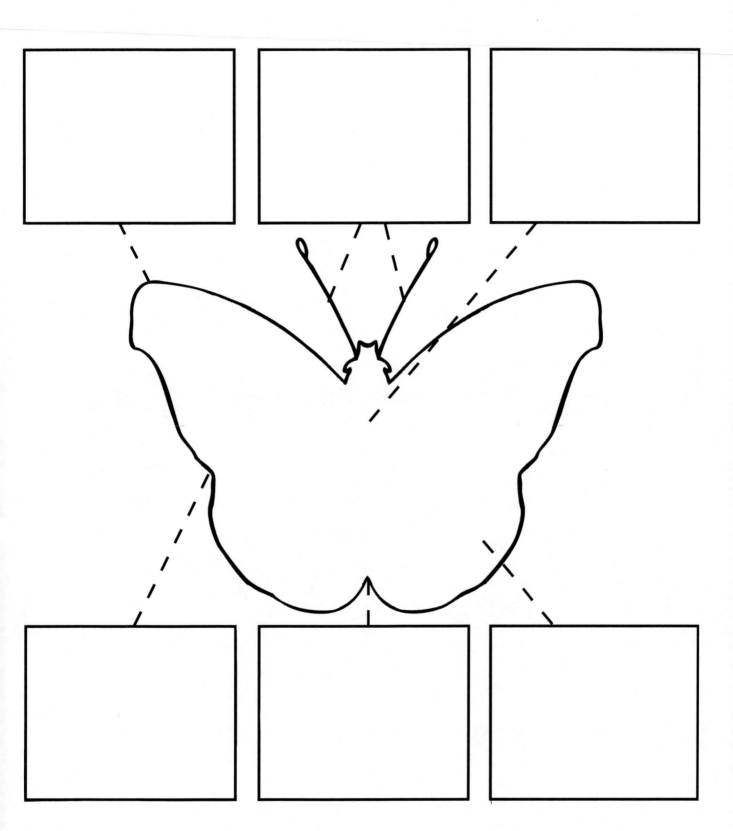

Write some information in the boxes about what you know about butterflies.

Write what you know

Pony	Puppy	Cat

Words to help
feed
water
clean out
exercise
care for

Fish	Hamster	Dinosaur

Elicit facts about each 'pet'. Re-write as a piece of informational writing using the annotated diagram as a plan.

Brilliant Activities for Creative Writing, Year 3
© Irene Yates and Brilliant Publications

Always

When I was
a child
I always wanted ...

... and I always
went ...

... and I always
thought ...

Write a poem like this:

I always wanted _____
and

I always went _____
and

I always thought _____
and

I always will be _____

Lots of talk to explore ideas. Aim for good expression of those ideas rather than rhyme or any of the poetry conventions. Share all poems aloud.

Food

Here are some adjectives to describe food. Use some of them to write a poem about what foods you like and dislike.

smelly	strong	soggy
crusty	squashy	delicious
healthy	crispy	mushy

Try:

Write a list poem; don't forget you could make a comment about your likes, dislikes and favourites etc at the end. **You could start like this ...**

Of all the foods in
all of the World,
the ones that
I most ...

Go through the words and gather others with the children noting down key words that they like the sound of. Encourage different starts and maybe surprise endings!

Brilliant Activities for Creative Writing, Year 3
© Irene Yates and Brilliant Publications

In the rainforest

Write a list poem of creatures in the rainforest, using alliteration, like this:

One slithery, slippery, slender snake
Two merry, mischievous, marvellous monkeys
Three ...

Lots of discussion about the rainforest and its inhabitants. Use the Internet to do more research about the different animals: how they live/eat/hunt. Work on developing adjectives and using alliteration. Make a class poem, display the work.

Simple sentences

Do this!

Choose a word – for instance, WORDS – and use the letters that form this word to be the start letter of each word you use in a sentence. So you could have: **We ordered red dance shoes.** For the word WHAT, you could have: **Who has a teapot?**

See how many sensible sentences you can create.

Tip:
Stick to small, short words, so that your sentences don't get too long.

Remember:
A sentence must have a verb in it.

Get individuals to suggest words. Do the task quickly, challenging children to work really fast and repeat many times.

Brilliant Activities for Creative Writing, Year 3
© Irene Yates and Brilliant Publications

Writing words that I understand

Narrative – another word for 'a narrative' is a story.
For example: A story telling us about 'Paul, the tortoise'.

Verb – a verb is a doing or action word.
For example: Paul, the tortoise, is **eating**.

Noun – a noun tells me the name of things/objects.
For example: Paul, the **tortoise**, is eating.

Proper noun – refers to someone or something's real name.
For example: **Paul**, the tortoise, is eating.

Article – an article is the 'a', 'an', 'the', 'this' or 'that' appearing before words.
For example: Paul, **the** tortoise, is eating.

Adverb – an adverb tells me When, Where or How something is done.
For example: Paul, the tortoise, is eating while his owner is **somewhere** in the garden.

Pronoun – a pronoun is a word that takes the place of a noun.
For example: Paul, the tortoise, is eating while **his** owner is in the garden.

Conjunctions – joins together words or groups of words.
For example: Paul, the tortoise, is eating **while** his owner is in the garden.

Prepositions – a preposition can tell us the position of something.
For example: **Paul**, the tortoise, is eating with his friends **in** the garden.

Sentence – a sentence is a group of words that makes sense and has a verb in it.
For example: Paul, the tortoise, is eating with his friends.

Adjectives – words used to describe a noun.
For example: **Paul**, the **brown and yellow** tortoise, is eating while his owner is in the garden.

Gathering ideas

Here's one way to find ideas:

Choose a subject, for example **playtime**. Write the word in the centre of your page, in a bubble. Now jot down anything that comes into your head as you look at that word. Once you have several words written down, concentrate your efforts on one of the newer words. Do the same thing on each word until you have a whole page of words. Lots of ideas will float into your head. Get writing before they float away again!

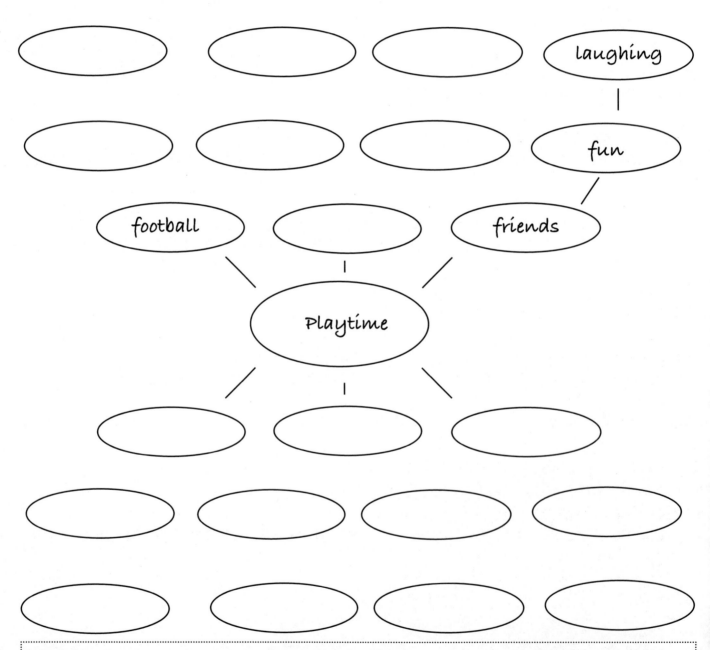

After talking about the page, do a whole class cluster, all together. The trick is not to listen to the logical left-hand-side of the brain, which tells the creative right-hand-side that it's being silly. Let it flow.

Brilliant Activities for Creative Writing, Year 3
© Irene Yates and Brilliant Publications

Plan sheet for writing instructions

Title:

- -

Goal: (This is what we want to do)

- -

- -

- -

Materials: (All the things we need to include)

- -

- -

- -

Method: (All the things we need to do in the right order!)

- -

- -

- -

- -

- -

- -

Comment: (This is what I want to say)

- -

- -

- -

Plan sheet for recount writing

Title:

Set the scene:
Opening paragraph, tell/write who, where, what, when, why

What happened? Put the events in the time order they occurred.
Event 1 _____

Event 2 _____

Event 3 _____

Event 4 _____

Event 5 _____

Ending comment:
I thought my trip was great because ...

Now use the plan sheet to write your recount.

Brilliant Activities for Creative Writing, Year 3
© Irene Yates and Brilliant Publications

Plan sheet for persuasive writing

Title:

Introduction:
(This is what it's all about)

- -

Viewpoint:
(This is your own feeling – whether you agree or disagree)

- -

- -

An argument or point to support your feeling.	A second argument or point to support your feeling.

A third argument or point to support your feeling.	A fourth argument or point to support your feeling.

A sentence about why you feel the opposite view is wrong.

- -

Sum up: I feel strongly that -

because ... -

Now, use the plan sheet to write your persuasive writing.

Plan sheet for writing a story

Sometimes a 'story' is called a 'narrative'.

Title:
- -

Where:
- -

When:
- -

Who:
- -

Main character details:
- -

What's the problem?
- -

What goes wrong? -

1. -

2. -

3. -

Resolution:
(How the problem is solved) -

Check and edit:

punctuation; spelling; nouns and pronouns; verbs; adjectives; adverbs; conjunctives.

Brilliant Activities for Creative Writing, Year 3
© Irene Yates and Brilliant Publications

Edit sheet for a story

Sometimes a 'story' is called a 'narrative'.

Title:
Check: **Where: When: What: Who: Why: How:** Are all these clear? If not add more.
Pronouns – have I stuck to one point-of-view all the way through? If it is written in the first person (I), have I kept to that throughout? If the story is in the third person, (he/she) have I kept to that? Mark any changes that need to be changed.
Verbs – have I used good strong active verbs all the way through? Mark any changes that need to be changed.
Tense – have I stuck to the same tense all the way through? Mark any changes that need to be changed.
Punctuation – have I used full stops and capital letters? Speech marks? Apostrophes? Paragraphs? Mark any changes that need to be changed.

Redraft sheet for story writing

Do I need to change my title?

If so, change to:

Do I need to change my viewpoint?
If so, change to:

Do I need to change the tenses of me verbs? (When)
Which ones?

How can I make the story a bit more exciting? Could I add a bit more?

Can I add a surprise?
How?

Have I described my main character well enough? (Who)
I can give a better description by ...

Is my setting clear enough? (Where)
I could describe it better if I ...

Is the ending good enough? A different ending might be ...

Now I'm ready to write another draft.

Brilliant Activities for Creative Writing, Year 3
© Irene Yates and Brilliant Publications

Perception of writing

....

When I write, I ...

- -

- -

- -

- -

- -

- -

This is me writing.

- -

- -

- -

Think about:
What kinds of writing you do
How you feel about writing and why you feel like that
What's important about your writing
What kind of writing you like best
Where your ideas come from
What do you want to happen to your writing.

Encourage individual, thoughtful responses. After writings are complete, lead a discussion about them. Encourage sharing where writers are willing.